FIELD TRIPS: A GUIDE FOR PLANNING AND CONDUCTING EDUCATIONAL EXPERIENCES

Wayne J. Krepel
Charles R. DuVall

PRAIRIE STATE COLLEGE
LEARNING CENTER

National Education Association
Washington, D.C.

Copyright © 1981
National Education Association of the United States
Stock No. 1683-1-00

Note

The opinions expressed in this publication should not be construed as representing the policy or position of the National Education Association. Materials published as part of the Analysis and Action Series are intended to be discussion documents for teachers who are concerned with specialized interests of the profession.

Library of Congress Cataloging in Publication Data

Krepel, Wayne J. 1933–
  Field trips.

  (Analysis and action series)
  Includes bibliographies.
  1. School excursions—Handbooks, manuals, etc.
I. DuVall, Charles R., 1929–   joint author.
II. Title. III. Series.
LB1047.K72   371.3'8   80-27823
ISBN 0-8106-1683-1

To the many students we have taught during our professional association with Indiana University at South Bend. We have profited greatly through the exchange of ideas with these students, and we hope that some of them are enriching their instruction through the use of the field trip.

CONTENTS

CHAPTER 1	USING FIELD TRIPS	7
	Terminology	7
	History of Field Trips	8
	Value of Field Trips	9
	School Board Policies	12
	Teacher Liability	13
	References	15
CHAPTER 2	CONDUCTING FIELD TRIPS	17
	Administrative Support	18
	Planning the Trip	18
	Working with the Host—Pupil-Teacher Planning—Teacher Responsibilities—Safety—Supervisory Assistance—Parental Permission—	
	The Trip	28
	Followup Activities	29
	Evaluating the Trip	30
	Checklist and Sample Form	31
	References	33
CHAPTER 3	IDEAS AND STRATEGIES	34
	Using Community Resources	34
	Locating Community Resources—	
	Subject-Oriented Trips	35
	Art—Career Education—Handicapped—Home Economics—Industrial Arts—Language Arts/English—Mathematics—Music—Science—Social Studies—Multidisciplinary Trips—International Travel—	
	Summary	51
	References	52
RECOMMENDED READINGS	....	54

The Authors
Wayne J. Krepel and Charles R. DuVall are Professors of Education, Indiana University at South Bend. Drs. Krepel and DuVall are also the co-authors of *Free Materials and Education* and *Education and Education-Related Serials: A Directory*.

The Advisory Panel
Edward L. Dejnozka, Head, Division of Administration and Personnel Services, College of Education, Florida Atlantic University, Boca Raton

Richard E. Erickson, social studies teacher, Marple Newtown School District, Newtown Square, Pennsylvania

Benjamin M. Hughes, teacher, Red Bluff Union High School, Red Bluff, California

Loretta M. Martin, President, North Carolina Association of Educators, Raleigh

Joyce Mercedes Smith, Associate Professor of Education, Georgia College, Milledgeville

Greg Stefanich, Associate Professor, Department of Curriculum and Instruction, University of Northern Iowa, Cedar Falls

CHAPTER 1
USING FIELD TRIPS

Field trips have taken varied forms over the years, ranging from the more traditional tours of local industries, "senior trips," and walking trips to help children become better acquainted with their neighborhoods, to trips crossing continents. They have also included trips during summer vacations, over weekends, and—in some cases—for the entire school year. They have used all types of transportation, from school bus and private automobile to airplanes, ships, and even mules. The only limitations on their use have been those imposed by the imagination and resourcefulness of the teacher. As "Auntie Mame" remarked to her nephew in the play *Mame*:

> Oh, my little love, your Auntie Mame is going to unlock doors for you. What adventures we're going to have together!
>
> Open a new window,
> Open a new door,
> Travel a new highway
> That's never been tried before . . . (Lawrence: 136)

TERMINOLOGY

Research of the literature reveals that the terminology describing this type of educational experience has changed over the years from the early writers' "school excursions," "school journeys," and "jaunts and journeys" to today's "educational tours," "educational trips," "field observation visits," "field trips," and "study tours." A recent definition of the field trip reads as follows:

> A trip arranged by the school and undertaken for educational purposes, in which students go to places where the materials of instruction may be observed and studied directly in their functional setting; for example, a trip to a factory, a city waterworks, a library, a museum, etc. Syn. instructional trip, school excursion, school journey; see plant tour. (Good: 239)

For the purposes of this publication, we will use the term *field trip* in its broadest sense.

HISTORY OF FIELD TRIPS

Historically, the field trip has its roots in the middle ages, when writers of that period recognized the inherent educational worth of travel, which usually followed the completion of formal schooling and was not an integral part of the educational program. Indeed, in even earlier times both Aristotle and Socrates recognized the value of travel as an educational experience.

The educational field trip as we know it today originated in Europe with the development of the excursion at the University of Jena under Stoy, modified and enlarged by Rein to make it an integral part of the total curriculum. From these beginnings, the field trip became directly associated with the teaching of subject matter in the educational program and the movement spread throughout Europe and Asia.

Writing in *School and Society* in 1935, Downs described an English secondary school master some 40 years earlier who, when discussing glaciers with his geography class, became aware that none of them, students or himself, had ever seen a glacier. This nameless visionary encouraged "his boys" to save a little money each week with the goal of taking a trip to Switzerland to see a glacier. Accordingly, at the end of the school year, some 60 boys and their masters took a month's educational excursion to Switzerland, marking the beginning of the "Continental School Journey," according to the chronicler (Downs: 541).

In another issue of *School and Society* in the same year, an unnamed correspondent for the *London Times* referred to the universal nature of educational excursions in the Japanese educational system of that era, noting that children took a great many journeys during the last two years of the elementary program (Correspondent: 300). The belief was that every child is a stranger in the world; thus it is the function of education to introduce the child to human and material surroundings. During this period the widespread use of the educational excursion was apparent in Belgium, Denmark, France, Germany, Holland, and Russia. Twenty years later, categorizing journeys as domestic trips taken during term time as well as trips abroad, Hall described excursions ranging from an airplane flight from Birmingham to London and back to study geography, to research expeditions to Lapland, Iceland, and British Columbia (Hall: 151–53).

The use of the field trip in the schools of the United States is of fairly recent origin. McKown and Roberts reported that schools in this country have always used trips to a limited extent, but noted that they tended to take the form of glorified school-picnic-type excursions. Despite common use of the term "excursions," therefore, these authors preferred "not to use it because it is too suggestive of a lark or a sight-seeing expedition, neither of which represents the school-trip idea" (McKown and Roberts: 181–82).

Writing in 1895, McMurry gave detailed instructions on the use of the field trip as an educational experience. His three-part procedure still constitutes the basic format for conducting field trips today: (1) preparation for the trip, (2) the trip itself, and (3) followup activities by teacher and class (McMurry: 14–15). Although its relative position or importance within the instructional program has varied—including use as an introduction to instruction, as the body of a unit of instruction, or as a culminating activity—the field trip is presently one of the most vibrant teaching-learning experiences available to educators. It may be a walk around the school yard and through a nearby woods; or it may be a visit to a firehouse or a meadow or across the continent or around the world (Howland: 1).

VALUE OF FIELD TRIPS

Although a number of values are attributed to field trips, their main objective is to provide learning through direct experience. The use of the community and its resources permits the expansion of the classroom to include the entire world of the pupil. The field trip is a laboratory which enables teachers to bridge the gap between the classroom and the world outside the school.

Among the values gained from these excursions are the provision of accurate firsthand information, the promotion of better citizenship, the opportunity for social training, the encouragement of love of travel, the formation of a connecting link between community and school, and the creation of interest (Curtis: 202).

Field trips increase student knowledge of a particular subject, but, even more importantly, they may increase the desire for knowledge. They add realism to a unit of study. Field trips help develop reading skills as pupils and teacher plan an outline of what they will do and see. They help students develop mapreading skills both during the planning stage and during the trip itself. They supply material for building a writing program, including reports and letters. They stimulate discussions. They require the use of mathematics to determine trip costs, supplies needed, and distance traveled.

Many early studies evaluated field trips in contrast with films or other audiovisual aids to learning. Recent studies have evaluated them within the total picture as one of many resources available to the teacher. Both types of evaluation are valid.

Field trips are generally evaluated by the individual teacher in a subjective manner, based on teacher observation of students. For example, Abraham analyzed the effectiveness of a student trip to Washington, D.C., concluding that the "effect of the visit was to increase esteem for the people who make, administer, and interpret the laws of the land" (Dale *et al*: 278). In addition to the use of observational data, several empirical studies are available which provide evaluative information regarding the field trip as an instructional tool.

One such study of 335 sixth grade pupils contained four units—Egypt, Printing, Transportation, and Communications. Clark carefully controlled the experiment so that nonexperimental factors would not affect the results. She administered interest and achievement tests and gave pupils the opportunity to write a one-page reaction to the unit. After tabulating and adjusting final scores for pretest scores and mental ages, she found the experimental (field trip) groups to be significantly superior in all units except Egypt, in which the control group was superior. No significant differences were reported between groups in absolute retention scores, except in the Printing unit, where the control group was found to be superior to one of the two experimental groups. No significant difference was found between groups in relative retention (Clark: 11–13). These results indicate the need for teachers to constantly evaluate field trips to achieve the desired outcomes.

In a study of eight 4B social studies classes, the findings were similar. The researcher concluded that a significantly greater degree of learning took place as a result of field trips, and reported no significant difference in the results of a retention test (Forster: 181).

Curtis studied 32 fifth graders divided into two groups to determine the contributions of field trips to their unit on soil erosion and conservation. He concluded that within certain stated limitations the excursions contributed to understanding when employed as a summary technique. Cautioning against undue expectations from the excursion per se, he recommended its use when an appropriate illustration of the unit of study is easily accessible in the community, and particularly when students' experiences are limited (Curtis: 202, 210).

Harvey examined the value of field trips for acquiring new knowledge and developing scientific attitudes rather than for illustrating or verifying information. Selecting two sections of ninth grade general science classes for the experiment and conservation as the unit of study, she concluded that the experimental (excursion) group showed an increase in scientific attitude which was of significant value. Her investigation proved that it was practical for these students to learn about a part of their environment using the scientific method. It also demonstrated that a worthwhile excursion can be conducted within a fifty-five minute class period (Harvey: 242–48).

The city of Milwaukee found a different use for field trips when it set up several orientation centers for new migrants and transients already within the city in 1960. Children who were culturally disadvantaged but who had normal ability were assigned to these centers for varying periods of time, usually one to four semesters. Because these children often lacked real-life experiences, the field trip was the focal point of their curriculum, providing activities at a concrete level, as well as a background of knowledge on which to build the conceptualization and abstract thinking skills so necessary for school success (Nuhlicek: 9).

A study of secondary school science field trips compared attributed values with empirically determined values and concluded that substantial experimental research is needed. It recommended, however, that, based upon available information, field trips should be used in the teaching of secondary science (Sorrentino and Bell: 235).

Another study, dealing with frequency and number of teachers taking pupils on field trips, reported that approximately 10 per cent of the teachers employed in a selected northern Indiana school district took field trips during a given school year (DuVall and Truex: 104). Additionally, Ayars surveyed 92 teachers who attended a community resources workshop to determine the reasons they did not use field trips with their classes. The reasons given, in descending order of frequency, were as follows: too full schedule, lack of transportation, too many pupils in classes, course of study requirements, time comsumed by routine duties, daily class schedule, problems of liability, too time consuming, and fear of disregarding some fundamental teaching. This researcher stated that extensive utilization was not likely to develop unless the administration provided favorable conditions, including an atmosphere encouraging the use of community resources (Ayars: 1).

As the preceding studies indicate, the field trip has been valued because of its contribution to learning. Thus the importance of selection, preparation, and conduct of the trip to ensure maximum benefit to students from this educational experience has been demonstrated.

SCHOOL BOARD POLICIES

The school board establishes policies covering the operation of the schools. These policies offer general statements of principle to administrators and staff relative to the conduct of the instructional program. From these policies administrative procedures evolve. It is the duty of the superintendent of schools to implement the policies through administrative procedures that will enable the professional staff to function effectively within the framework established by the board.

Despite an almost total lack of state statutes dealing with field trips and their educational value, there are in existence school board policies and procedures covering the conduct of field trips. Recent research studies have revealed the following information:

1. Most school districts have policies, either written or unwritten, which permit the use of the educational field trip by their instructional staff.

2. In most cases the responsibility for determining the acceptability of field trip sites rests with the individual building principal and/or teacher. Many times this is a shared responsibility.

3. In the identification of criteria for determining the acceptability of field trip sites, the most frequently indicated criterion was that the field trip must be educationally significant and suitable. Other criteria cited were distance (accessibility), administrator or teacher judgment, relationship to maturity level of pupils, and safety.

4. School buses, public transportation, and walking were the most frequently indicated acceptable means of transportation for use in field trips (Krepel and DuVall; and Krepel).

In most school districts the teacher handbook provides information regarding board policy and administrative procedures related to the conduct of field trips. Many of these handbooks deal extensively with the topic. In other districts separate publications covering only the subject of field trips are available. In any case, it is usually advisable for teachers to check with their principals regarding administrative procedures covering these instructional ventures.

TEACHER LIABILITY

It is important that teachers be aware of their legal responsibilities during field trips. Conditions outside the classroom may increase the element of danger to pupils. Children may expect more freedom away from the school environment, when in reality some field trips may necessitate greater restrictions than those normally required in the regular classroom. Consequently, more careful teacher supervision may be appropriate.

In particular, the transportation of students to and from the site of the field trip may be a cause of concern. Questions regarding the use of school buses and other vehicles, including public transportation and privately owned automobiles, have arisen. Some schools may not, and in certain cases cannot, provide transportation, thus creating problems for teachers wishing to use the field trip as an instructional aid.

A study of teacher liability by the authors surveying all state superintendents of public instruction, attorneys general, and legal officers of the several state education associations examined state laws and court cases. Its conclusions were as follows:

> The findings concerning the existence of specific state laws dealing with teacher responsibility and liability in the matter of field trips disclosed that such laws are few in number. Only three states (California, Illinois, and Kentucky) had laws which could clearly be identified in this category.
>
> Of the court decisions concerning field trip responsibility and liability, only one case, which arose in California, was recent enough to be classified as a positive response. Several other states noted either opinions of legal or administrative officers or earlier court decisions, the relevance of which was discussed.
>
> Many comments were received from the respondents. Most frequently stated was the opinion that the legal standard of reasonable care is the same on a field trip as it is in the regular classroom. Of course, the teacher should exercise that degree of care that a normally prudent person would exercise under similar circumstances. This "prudence" may well mean that a higher degree of care would be exercised on a field trip, under circumstances prevailing in the given situation, than would normally be expected in the "protected environment" of the classroom. Thus, the teacher is subject to no greater tort liability on a field trip than when performing duties in the classroom if reasonable care and foresight are exercised. (DuVall and Krepel 1978: 24)

An earlier study of the same state offices reported similar findings. In addition, it noted that in many states liability insurance is available to teachers through governmental agencies and/or membership in professional organizations (DuVall and Krepel 1972: 648).

Because of challenges to the school district's traditional immunity from tort liability—an immunity based on that of the king of England in 1765—teachers and other school officials today may be sued and may be held liable for injuries to pupils not only in the conduct of field trips but at any time. In many cases state governments have eliminated sovereign immunity as a protective device for school districts with the enactment of "save harmless" laws by approximately one-third of the states. For example, the New York statute requires the board of education to "indemnify all its employees against financial loss for acts of negligence committed in the line of duty" (Wetterer: 530). Such laws differ from state to state, some permitting and others requiring the school district to reimburse employees who are held liable for injuries resulting from negligence.

Liability for an accident may be found when negligence is involved. One criterion often used to determine negligent conduct is foreseeability. For instance, if a reasonably prudent person could have foreseen the consequences of an act or would have acted differently under the circumstances and the teacher failed in this respect, then the latter may have been negligent. On the other hand, a teacher is usually free of blame if an injury is caused by an unavoidable or unforeseeable accident.

Some state statutes require or permit school districts to carry liability insurance. Grieve described a pertinent example involving both the "save harmless" clause and liability insurance. In this case, a teacher and his student passengers en route to a music festival in a school station wagon were all killed in an accident. Subsequent litigation revealed negligence on the part of the driver. Due to the state's "save harmless" statute, the school district was held responsible for the action of the teacher. However, the liability insurance carried by the district was insufficient to cover the enormous claims. Consequently, the district increased the tax rate for several years to settle the claims resulting from the tragedy (Grieve: 86).

Professional organizations often provide liability insurance through group plans for all members. Such coverage may be available for a small fee or it may be a benefit of membership. It may include payment of all attorney fees and other costs, as well as payment of judgments within maximum limits, depending upon the group contract.

To ensure student safety and to avoid teacher liability, the following areas merit special attention:

1. *Supervision of students.* Inadequate supervision, in the event of an injury, may be a factor in determining teacher negligence. The court may rule that the presence of a teacher may have prevented the accident. Therefore, it is usually recommended that a teacher not leave a classroom or playground unsupervised. It is expected that teachers will provide reasonable supervision, but the courts do not require constant scrutiny.

2. *Transporting students to and from activities away from the school site.* Some states have specific statutes authorizing school districts to provide transportation for such activities. Some states also allow school districts to purchase liability insurance for transportation purposes only, an indication that districts are concerned about accidents while transporting students.

3. *The use of privately owned automobiles for transporting students.* The teacher or owner may be found liable for injuries to students riding in such vehicles (Howard: 413).

4. *Permission slips.* Although required for field trips, such forms signed by a parent or guardian do not relieve teachers of responsibility for pupils, as both Phlegar and Howard emphasized. They simply inform the parent or guardian of the trip or indicate parental permission for the pupil to engage in the educational activity (Phlegar: 22; Howard: 413).

The next chapter discusses these topics in greater detail.

To conclude, then, regardless of "save harmless" laws and liability insurance, a study of the literature reveals the need for teachers to take extra precautions while involved with students on field trips. A consideration of the maturity, age, and physical condition of students, together with careful planning and adequate supervision, will serve not only to ensure reasonable care but to promote maximum student learning and enjoyment during these educational activities away from school.

REFERENCES

Ayars, Albert L. "The Community Resources Workshop: Project in School-Community Cooperation." Undated one-page pamphlet. Hill & Knowlton, Inc., Education Department, 150 East 42d Street, New York, N.Y.

Clark, Etta Callista. "An Experimental Evaluation of the School Excursion." *Journal of Experimental Education* 12:10–19; September 1943.

Correspondent of *London Times Educational Supplement*. "School Journeys in Japan." *School and Society* 42:300–301; August 31, 1935.

Curtis, Dwight K. "The Contributions of the Excursion to Understanding." *Journal of Educational Research* 38:201–11; November 1944.

Dale, Edgar; Finn, J. D.; and Hoban, C. F. "Research of Audio-Visual Materials." *National Society for the Study of Education,* 48th Yearbook, Part I. Chicago: University of Chicago Press, 1949.

Downs, S. W. "The School Journey Movement in Great Britain." *School and Society* 42:541–42; October 19, 1935.

DuVall, Charles R., and Krepel, Wayne J. "Teacher Liability During Field Trips." *Journal of Law and Education* 1:637–48; October 1972.

———, and ———. "Laws and Court Cases Related to Field Trips." *NOLPE School Law Journal* 8:14–24; vol. 1, 1978.

———, and Truex, Donald Walter. "Computerized Community Resources Handbook: A Joint Project of Indiana University at South Bend and the South Bend Community School Corporation." *Research in Education* 6:131; April 1971 (ED 045 481).

Forster, Edith C. "An Evaluation of the Field Trip in the Formation of Social Concepts and Generalizations." *Dissertation Abstracts* 22:181; July–September 1961.

Good, Carter V., ed., *Dictionary of Education*. 3d ed. New York: McGraw-Hill, 1973.

Grieve, Andrew. "Legal Aspects of Transportation for Athletic Events." *Athletic Journal* 47:64+; March 1967.

Hall, Wendy. "School Journeys in British Education." *School and Society* 82:151–53; November 12, 1955.

Harvey, Helen W. "An Experimental Study of the Effect of Field Trips upon the Development of Scientific Attitudes in a Ninth Grade General Science Class." *Science Education* 35:242–48; December 1951.

Howard, Alvin W. "Teacher Liability and the Law." *Clearing House* 42:411–13; March 1968.

Howland, Adelene E. *How to Conduct a Field Trip*. National Council for the Social Studies, "How to Do It Series," no. 12. Washington, D.C.: National Education Association, 1958.

Krepel, Wayne J. "A Survey of School Board Policies and Administrative Procedures for Dealing with Field Trips in Selected Smaller School Districts in the United States." *Research in Education* 9:62; August 1974 (ED 089 399).

———, and DuVall, Charles R. "A Survey of School Board Policies and Administrative Procedures for Dealing with Field Trips in School Districts in Cities with Populations over 100,000 in the United States." *Research in Education* 8:30; January 1973 (ED 066 810).

Lawrence, Jerome; Lee, Robert E.; and Herman, Jerry. *Mame*. New York: Random House, 1967.

McKown, Harry C., and Roberts, Alvin B. *Audio-Visual Aids to Instruction.* "School Trips and Tours" (chapter 9, pp. 181–210). New York: McGraw-Hill Book Co., 1940.

McMurry, Charles A. *Special Method in Geography.* 2d ed. Bloomington, Ill.: Public School Publishing Co., 1895.

Nuhlicek, Allen L. "Orientation Centers for In-Migrants and Transients." *Education Digest* 32:8–11; April 1967.

Phlegar, Frederick L. "School Law and the Teacher." *Virginia Journal of Education* 60:20–22; May 1967.

Sorrentino, Anthony V., and Bell, Paul E. "A Comparison of Attributed Values with Empirically Determined Values of Secondary School Science Field Trips." *Science Education* 54:233–36; July 1970.

Wetterer, Charles M. "Can He Be Sued? An Evaluator's Dilemma." *Clearing House* 40:529–31; May 1966.

CHAPTER 2
CONDUCTING FIELD TRIPS

The foregoing discussion of the legal aspects of field trips should not discourage teachers from taking pupils outside the "safe" confines of the classroom. It was intended to increase teacher awareness of legal liability. Field trips are instructionally acceptable. As previously noted, most boards of education approve of them as a means of acquiring a desired diversity in the educational program. Adopted board policies offer concrete proof of this acceptability.

In addition to board policy, many schools have specific procedures for conducting field trips, usually contained in the teacher's handbook. Most familiar among these procedures are the form for teacher completion to obtain administrative approval for the trip and the prescribed "parental permission slip" provided by many districts. The existence of community resources handbooks or recommended lists of places suitable for class visitation offers further evidence of school district approval.

The field trip is treated separately from those educational experiences which take place on a day-to-day basis because it normally takes place outside the classroom. Teachers often believe they have more responsibilities while conducting a field trip than when conducting a lesson in their regular classroom, but this belief is not true. The responsibilities differ in kind, not in degree, from those encountered in the classroom. Because the welfare of the pupil is always the principal concern, teachers are subject to a doctrine of prudence or reasonableness in the conduct of all their classes. On a field trip the only difference is that instruction is taking place in a less protected environment. The following guidelines are intended to help teachers prepare for and conduct field trips safely and in an educationally meaningful manner.

ADMINISTRATIVE SUPPORT

Discuss, in detail, any proposed field trip with the principal. The first and most important consideration to discuss is the educational value of the trip. Once the educational justification is established, the remaining details will follow with relative ease. It is probably a good idea to write out objectives in order to facilitate communication with the principal, and later with the host and students. In addition, these objectives will later focus the post-trip evaluation upon desired outcomes.

Become acquainted with school board policies and/or administrative procedures covering the conduct of field trips. These may include such items as the determination of site acceptability, scheduling limitations (caused by bus schedule requirements), and many other details.

Another matter to determine during this early planning stage is the availability or existence of liability insurance. This item may be covered by an insurance policy carried by the board, a policy carried on the bus which includes provision for field trips, the teacher's or district's liability contract, or the purchase of a rider (usually at a nominal cost) to an already existing insurance policy.

PLANNING THE TRIP

Three essential ingredients required to plan any field trip are the following: (1) the host, who must be involved early in the process; (2) the pupils, who must be involved continuously because it is their trip; and (3) the teacher, who must act as a catalytic agent throughout the process, constantly coordinating all aspects of the trip as well as taking care of the myriad logistical details which arise.

Working with the Host

Hosts have much to offer. It is therefore prudent to involve them in the planning stage to benefit from their ideas and suggestions as well as from those of teacher and pupils. An opportunity should exist for host and teacher to meet before the visit to share ideas and plans, discussing such matters as guide arrangements, safety rules and regulations, use of cameras, food and drink regulations, and provisions for handicapped students. The teacher may also wish to invite the host to visit the classroom for planning the trip, or as part of the followup activities.

It is suggested that the teacher make the initial contact with the host. Although pupil involvement in planning is certainly recommended, the initial contact should be entrusted to someone who can make commitments for the group, and usually that person is the teacher. It is well to have several possible dates available, in the event that the first suggested date is not acceptable to the host. If the class is to visit several sites on the same trip, then it will be necessary to work out logistical problems in cooperation with the several hosts, including a tentative timetable taking into account driving or walking distances, traffic conditions, and other details.

Consider the provisions for taking handicapped pupils in the group on field trips. Rather than exclude a handicapped pupil, plan the trip with this special needs pupil in mind. The requirements to be met by host institutions will vary with the type of handicapping condition to be served. For instance, students in wheelchairs require ramps. If they are not available at a trip site, then schedule an alternative location. In many cases the parent will be happy to accompany the child and to provide any needed assistance.

After the planning visit, confirm in writing to the host the day, date, and time of the trip, and any other necessary details. Such a letter reassures the host of teacher interest and provides teacher and students an opportunity to ask additional questions. It also guards against the possibility of the group walking in and saying, "Surprise! We're here!!!"

Pupil-Teacher Planning

Schedule adequate planning sessions with pupils so that they may be active participants in this educational activity. While working with the host, involve the class. Encourage students to collect additional data prior to the trip and to formulate questions to be answered at the site.

The group may choose to use audiovisual aids such as slides and videotapes to aid these planning efforts. Special reports and class-conducted research may be part of the process. Other decisions directly concerning pupils are those related to pictures and the use of cameras, note-taking procedures (e.g., different teams might share the responsibility for an area of expertise), and safety precautions.

In other words, involve the class in all decisions not in conflict with the safety or overall scheduling requirements of the trip. Such decisions should also be consistent with board policy, school procedure, and sound pedagogical practice, since the final responsibility for the success or failure of this educational activity is and must be the teacher's.

Table 1 presents a schema for instructional organization and class involvement, an educational process which may be accomplished in a

TABLE 1

Comparison of Three Organized Patterns of Instruction*

	Teacher Role	Student Role	Possible Advantages	Possible Disadvantages
TEACHER-ORIENTED	(a) Selects the problem, objectives, and concepts. (b) Directs student observation and data gathering personally. (c) Assigns responsibilities for completion of tasks according to knowledge of individual differences.	(a) Follows directions and records data suggested by teacher. (b) Analyzes data and draws conclusions.	(a) More detailed observations possible because teacher selects ideal specimens for study. (b) Much of trial and error of learning eliminated. More efficient from standpoint of time and amount of material covered. (c) More concepts revealed in sequential fashion.	(a) Range of observation limited largely to teacher's ability to select items. (b) Little opportunity for students to select relevant objects and information and reject irrelevancies. (c) Large pupil-teacher ratio. (d) Spontaneous and unplanned learning less likely to occur.

* From "Conducting a Field Trip: Organizational Patterns for Instruction" by Clifford E. Knapp. Reproduced with permission from *Science and Children,* September 1970. Copyright 1970 by the National Science Teachers Association, 1742 Connecticut Ave., NW, Washington, D.C. 20009.

	Teacher Role	Student Role	Possible Advantages	Possible Disadvantages
MODIFIED	(a) Selects important characteristics for observation by constructing a data sheet. (b) Divides the class into small groups and establishes physical boundaries for investigation. (c) Anticipates learning barriers and attempts to prepare the students in classroom for solving problem and meeting objective. (d) Circulates among groups and facilitates learning.	(a) Selects and observes appropriate specimens for observation. (b) Records data. (c) Demonstrates maturity and self-discipline in meeting designated task.	(a) Students may cooperatively solve problem and benefit from varied abilities of group members. (b) Students may work at their own pace. (c) The teacher can provide more individual attention in identifying and solving student problems.	(a) Students may not select the best specimen examples for examination. (b) Students may encounter problems which the teacher is unable to assist in solving. (c) Some students may not function well in self-directed learning situations.
STUDENT-ORIENTED	(a) Establishes boundaries of time, location, and student behavior. (b) Motivates students and presents preparation and follow-up activities.	(a) Clarifies task, establishes a plan for problem solution and meets human interaction situations that may hinder group effectiveness. (b) Plans to communicate findings to class.	(a) Provides for maximum application of creative thinking and group involvement situations. (b) Students can pursue aspects of the problem which interest them.	(a) Effectiveness is dependent upon the ability and motivation of the group participants. (b) Difficult to execute if all students are expected to adopt this pattern rapidly.

number of ways. The schema outlines three possible approaches ranging from strongly teacher-oriented to fully student-oriented (Knapp: 27). The approach to be used is a decision to be made by the teacher directly involved in the field trip.

A student teacher may also be a member of the "instructional team." If this is the case, he/she should participate in planning from the beginning. In fact, the supervising teacher, although ultimately responsible, may assign much of the planning to the student teacher in order to provide experience in this area of instruction. For detailed procedures of student teacher involvement with field trip planning and execution, see the article "Field Trips and the Secondary Student Teacher" in *The Teacher Educator* (Krepel: 27–30).

Teacher Responsibilities

The teacher should know exactly what educational benefits are available to pupils from a visit to a particular organization or site. In other words, it is the teacher's professional and ethical responsibility to be sure that the trip will be a wise expenditure of valuable class time.

While previewing the site and discussing the forthcoming visit with the host, it may be helpful to take notes. Such notes may take forms other than the traditional pad-and-pencil-type. One very effective way to aid recall is by taking slides or snapshots. Slides are recommended because they can be easily used with the entire class. Prints, if needed, can then be made from slides at a relatively low cost. Another form of note-taking is through the use of the video transcription recorder (VTR), a method which has been used with success for this purpose (DuVall: 279–80).

The following is a list of teacher responsibilities during preliminary planning.

1. Inform the host of the educational objectives. Write, or have students write, a letter containing specific questions.
2. Discuss time limitations with the host. These constraints may occur because of the nature of the tour, bus availability, school schedule, and other planned visits.
3. Identify potential dangers (see "Safety").
4. Note special clothing requirements. This problem may be tied in with the existence of potential dangers. One example is the wearing of loose, sloppy clothing when visiting a plant containing moving machinery in which clothing may become entangled.
5. Check regulations concerning food and drink. On a trip taken several years ago by one of the authors when the host announced that the canteen was available to the class to purchase soft drinks and candy, the tour immediately lost much of its

educational value as students became more interested in making purchases than in the host's presentation. To avoid this problem, schedule a "rest break" which may include a canteen stop. Fatigue may be more of a factor on a field trip than in the classroom; therefore such breaks are necessary.

6. Arrange for restroom stops. Public accommodations are usually best; a telephone call to the park department will confirm their availability. Because some park restrooms may be closed at various times of the day or during certain seasons, this procedure is strongly recommended. If public facilities are not available, the teacher may be able to make arrangements with a host. In such cases, an examination of restroom facilities is advisable, both for cleanliness and for a check on scheduling. For example, the scheduling of a student restroom break at the same time as the plant coffee break would greatly inconvenience both students and workers. A little attention to the plant schedule can avoid this type of situation. As a final resort, the teacher may be able to make arrangements with one or more gasoline service station operators along the route. Keep in mind that not all service station proprietors view the descent of a busload of eager pupils upon their restrooms as a blessing. For this reason it is a good idea to make prior arrangements.

7. Check to determine if the host has more than one group scheduled for a visit at the same time. Such planning is the host's prerogative. If the host schedules more than one group, however, students are sometimes more interested in talking with their peers from other schools than in the conduct of their own trip. Staggered scheduling can avoid many potential problems of this nature.

8. Consider the necessity of eating meals on a long trip. If the group decides to carry sack lunches, suggest to parents that students not bring along easily spoiled foods unless facilities for refrigeration are available. Cooling facilities will be necessary for milk, for example. (One or two portable ice chests will usually suffice.) To avoid the possibility of upset stomachs, substitute water or a bland drink for milk. In addition, several large brown grocery bags are useful for disposing of garbage and for pupils who become bus sick.

9. Be sure to have a first aid kit available on the trip, and to be acquainted with the basic principles of first aid. If the group is going into a region known to be inhabited by poisonous snakes, then also include a snakebite kit. While the danger of snakes is remote in certain parts of the country, it can be a reality in others. Indeed, California law covering field trips contains a provision requiring that snakebite kits be taken on all such trips.

Safety

The practice of prior planning cannot be overemphasized when safety is involved. Teacher-pupil planning can help students understand that their safety is of the utmost importance not only to the teacher, but also to themselves. A few illustrations will explain this concern, and at the same time suggest appropriate methods for handling it.

Although teachers are responsible for the accounting of pupils, a method of accomplishing this accounting may be a matter for group planning. First, the teacher should stress the importance of pupils staying together. Then, the class may consider the buddy system or proceeding as an intact group. In the buddy system each person has a partner and the two students stay together throughout the trip. For ease of checking, pupils may wish to have assigned seats on the bus, and for fairness they should alternate window seats on a predetermined schedule. It is advisable that partners be of the same sex so that, for safety reasons, they may go to the restroom together.

Discuss frankly with students the proper way to handle advances from deviates in public restrooms. Do not ignore the problem; rather, discuss it in the nonthreatening atmosphere of the classroom prior to departure. One method of controlling potential problems is to stress that pupils never go to restrooms alone, only with their "buddy." Instruct students not to talk to strangers, and to withdraw immediately from the restroom if approached by an unfamiliar person, reporting such behavior to the adult in charge.

During the conduct of the tour at the host institution it may be advantageous to subdivide the class into smaller groups. Previously assigned groups (by color code, type of hat worn, or numbers such as odd-even or 1–10, 11–20, and 21 plus) make this a simple matter on site. With younger pupils, it may be advisable to have even closer control than with older ones. One method uses a clothesline knotted every three feet with a knot assigned to each child. Thus it is possible to have 25 children following one leader with little difficulty and a maximum of control.

Another concern is crossing streets. The teacher may wish to ask help from the local police or school crossing guards, or to train selected pupils to help with this most important task. If given sufficient time to process the request and arrange schedules, the local police are normally most cooperative. In field trips conducted by the authors the local police assisted many times. In one instance, a uniformed officer was assigned to accompany the trip. On other trips patrol cars and officers located at difficult crossing sites assisted the teacher. The only requirement imposed was to provide the police department an itinerary and an idea of the approximate time the assistance was needed.

In planning walking trips, use sidewalks where available, even if this means taking a less direct route. Potential dangers while walking include parking lot entrances to supermarkets and shopping plazas; delivery docks; and entrances to alleys and private garages and driveways. If the walking trip requires crossing private property, such as going into a field for nature study, be sure to obtain written permission from the owner. Prior to the trip, go over the route specifically looking for bogs, hazardous precipices, and other natural dangers.

The use of buses or other forms of public transportation encompasses another set of safety factors. Choose a predetermined place for boarding and disembarking from a bus. Special bus parking can be arranged at the site. In many cases the host will take care of these arrangements, while in others the teacher may wish to contact the local police department to have parking space reserved on the street. Often the police will place No Parking signs along the curb or cover parking meters well in advance of the arrival of the bus.

A matter of special concern in the use of bus transportation is the different pattern of safety behavior required by pupils when using public transportation. Most states require all traffic to halt when students board or leave a school bus. In no case is traffic required to halt when they use public transportation. Thus the teacher will have to instruct children in an entirely different pattern of behavioral responses when using public transportation.

The use of school or public transportation is recommended for field trips. Insurance coverage and driver licensing requirements for both school and public buses are designed to ensure safe transportation for large numbers of persons. It is difficult to determine the appropriate amount of liability insurance coverage required for privately owned vehicles used in field trip transportation. In addition, drivers of privately owned vehicles seldom have the type of driver's license required to transport pupils on such trips. Both of these factors are potential sources of difficulty.

Encourage students to develop basic rules of conduct to follow during the field trip. By means of teacher-pupil planning, the class can consider all aspects of discipline problems and determine acceptable modes of behavior. These rules should encompass school board policies and building procedures, as well as any safety precautions which the host institution expects to be observed. After the teacher explains the contraints under which the group will be operating, it is the students' responsibility to determine the course of action desired, operating within these constraints. As with most aspects of group planning, the decisions reached may require compromises.

The safety precautions to be observed on the site of the visit are usually well defined by the host. (If the host does not broach the subject during the pre-visit, the teacher should bring it up.) The nature of the site may well determine such factors as the type of clothing worn and the size of the group. For example, if the site has a large number of machines, the host may forbid the wearing of loose, flowing clothing. This rule might prevent pupils from dressing in shawl-type sweaters, neckties, loose shirts and blouses. Certain types of shoes, such as those with extremely high heels or platform soles, may constitute another safety hazard. The host may also wish to have students subdivided into smaller groups for the tour. In such cases, the teacher should arrange for additional adult supervisory help so that each student group will be accompanied by one adult from the school as well as the host's guide. These aides should be involved in the training and planning sessions well in advance of the trip.

If we appear to have overemphasized safety, we believe this concern is warranted. We have cited specific examples of safety precautions not because a greater degree of caution must be exercised on the field trip than in the regular classroom, but rather to point out the kind of precautions to be taken. The classroom atmosphere is more familiar than that encountered on the field trip. One might argue that in the normal classroom the precautions necessary to ensure against a pupil being hit by a truck are minimal while on the field trip the danger is more real and present. But if a teacher removes a student from the classroom because of unacceptable behavior, requiring her/him to stand unsupervised in the hall, there may be a risk of which the teacher is not aware. In other words, whether in the classroom or outside of it, during the school day it is the teacher's responsibility to take adequate precautions to ensure the safety of students.

Supervisory Assistance

Additional supervisory helpers may include teacher aides, parents, other teachers (particularly resource teachers whose specialty may be involved), the principal, or members of the custodial staff. The number and type of such helpers needed depend upon the nature of the field trip. In many cases the host may make suggestions or may supply additional supervisory assistance on the site. But the provision of adequate supervisory help is the teacher's responsibility. Common sense is a guide in this matter. As previously mentioned, one adult supervisor should accompany each subgroup on the entire trip.

Be sure that the additional supervisors receive adequate training, as necessary, to familiarize them with the educational objectives and implementation of the trip. One way to accomplish this is to involve them in the entire planning process. Such involvement will give them a sense of their value in the undertaking; it will also accustom students to their presence and participation in all phases of the trip.

Parental Permission

The permission slip or consent form is a statement that the pupil (specified by name) has permission from a parent or guardian to participate in the field trip. (See the sample form at the end of this chapter.) In addition to giving specifics of the trip, the form should contain the name and telephone number of the person to contact in the event of an emergency, as well as permission for emergency medical treatment. It should also include directions from the parent or guardian regarding the use of any necessary prescription drugs. While the need for this last type of information seldom develops, it gives a sense of security to have it available. Therefore we recommend that the teacher carry the permission slips on the trip. Finally, the form should contain a space for the parent or guardian's signature and the date.

A permission slip signed by a parent or guardian should be required of each student for each field trip. No pupil should be permitted to participate in a field trip unless a signed permission slip is in the teacher's possession before leaving the school building at the time of the trip. Verbal authorization—by telephone or in person—should never be accepted. Although the signed form in no way relieves the teacher of any responsibility for the student while on the trip, it is important because it is a way of ensuring that the parent is aware that the student will be away from the school at the time designated and will be at the place(s) indicated.

The permission slip should be accompanied by a cover letter explaining to parents the nature of the field trip—its educational purpose, the complete itinerary (including approximate times for arrival and departure from each site), any costs involved, clothing and special requirements, and a suggestion concerning the amount of spending money (based on a group decision made during the teacher-pupil planning).

If the permission statement is appended to the descriptive letter, students should detach it and return it to the teacher. Parents may retain the cover letter for information purposes. The signed permission slip assures the teacher (insofar as it is practically possible) that the trip information is in the hands of the parent. It says that the parent, in effect, approves of the educational purposes and supports this venture. The courts have viewed the use of a signed permission slip as one example of the teacher's exercise of sound judgment and competence, but not as a waiver of responsibility.

Some students may not receive permission from their parents to accompany the group on the field trip; others may forget their signed slips. These students should not be permitted to make the trip; they should be left behind with another teacher. As mentioned before, under no circumstances should the teacher accept verbal permission or authorization. If a large number of students must be left behind, then consider requesting the services of a substitute teacher or cancelling the trip because of lack of interest.

THE TRIP

The trip should be rewarding to all participants. The planning that involved host, pupils, teacher, and supervisory assistants should now result in a meaningful educational experience based upon the originally stated objectives. On the day of the trip final details include checking the list of participants prior to departure, reminding students of the rules of conduct previously agreed upon, and conducting an inventory of food and equipment. Also, be sure to have the school's telephone number readily available. After reaching the site, the host becomes responsible for the tour itself. But the teacher must be available to help when necessary and to keep the tour on schedule.

During the trip students should have the opportunity to ask questions and make notes, and, when appropriate, to take pictures and obtain brochures or literature. Notes taken by means of a portable audio or video tape recorder will assist the followup classroom discussion.

In the event of an emergency during the trip, the advance preparations will prove invaluable—especially the permission slips with emergency instructions, the first aid kit, the prescriptive drug information, and the extra aides.

At the end of each visit while still at the site, we recommend a session for questions, answers, and discussion. At this time the host can offer final explanations and clarifications. Finally, this is also the time for the group to express appreciation and personal thanks for the host's contributions.

FOLLOWUP ACTIVITIES

Upon returning to school, teachers have an opportunity to reinforce the learning experience of the field trip by means of followup activities. Among the many different forms of such activities are the following:

1. *Discussions.* The teacher may initiate a discussion of the sites visited on the bus as the pupils travel from one site to the next, or on the return trip following the last visit. On a walking trip, the discussion may take place on site as well as while walking between sites.

2. *Cameras.* Instant types, in particular, will enhance immediate discussion activities. Subsequent sharing of pictures from other cameras will help recall the experiences of the trip over the next several weeks. To aid this sharing pupils can post their snapshots on the bulletin board where these mementos of the trip will stimulate spontaneous discussion.

3. *Video tape recorders (VTR).* If the teacher has used the VTR unit to record the trip in advance, or has taken it along on the trip, he/she may replay the tape for reinforcement. An interesting activity is to compare snapshots taken by students with the VTR pictures to illustrate what teacher and students viewed as important.

4. *Formal writing assignments.* Students may choose the site or activity which most impressed them and write a brief descrip-

tion of it. Then they select several of these papers to include with the thank you letter to the host.

5. *Bulletin board displays.* Using the most interesting memorabilia acquired in the course of the trip—including brochures and other materials provided by the host—such displays are useful learning activities. If, as occasionally happens, a student "acquires" a souvenir of value to the host, teacher and student should return the "souvenir" with appropriate apologies. Such an incident can serve as an opportunity for teaching values concerning the property rights of others.

6. *Thank you letters.* This is another opportunity for the class to engage in a useful writing activity. All pupils need not write letters; but if they do, send only the best ones to the host.

EVALUATING THE TRIP

The final step of the field trip is an honest appraisal of its educational value, which includes a listing of strengths, weaknesses, and suggestions for improvement. The evaluation should be based on the educational objectives formulated during the planning stage. These objectives provide an excellent means of judging the effectiveness of the experience. Questions that may be asked include the following:

Did the trip accomplish its objectives?
Were all pupil questions answered?
Was additional unanticipated information gained?
If I knew then what I know now, would I take the same trip again?

It is hoped that the answers to such questions will be yes. If not, then one more question should be asked:

What could I have done to make the field trip a success?

Consider any suggested improvements before initiating the next trip.

A written evaluation of the field trip should become part of the teacher's instructional file. It should be shared with students (who helped prepare for the trip), with the host (who helped plan it), and with the building principal (who initially approved it). If changes are necessary, the evaluation will indicate the improvements needed for future trips. Honest evaluations will lead to improved trips and ultimately to improved education.

CHECKLIST AND SAMPLE FORM

Finally, amidst all the "shalts" and "shalt nots," remember that the field trip is an educational experience. It provides an opportunity for firsthand, rather than vicarious, learning.

Teachers, administrators, and boards of education have developed numerous checklists to help make trips true learning experiences. Any such list—with variations made to suit individual needs—may help avoid unnecessary problems and delays. The following checklist and sample consent form are presented for information purposes. Teachers may reproduce them without seeking release from the copyright holder.

FIELD TRIP CHECKLIST

__ Educational Objectives identified
__ Tentative date set
__ Administrative approval obtained
__ Host contacted
__ Preview site visit by teacher

Discussion with host and pupils concerning:

Host	Pupils	Item
__	__	Educational objectives
__	__	Safety rules
__	__	Pupil conduct
__	__	Use of cameras, VTR, etc.
__	__	Food and drink regulations
__	__	Special clothing
__	__	Guide arrangements and authority
__	__	Provision for handicapped pupils

__ Confirmation letter to host
__ Confirmation letter received from host
__ Supervisory helpers identified
__ Restroom reservations completed
__ Eating arrangements completed
__ Bus arrangements completed
__ Insurance clearance completed
__ Route cleared (police assistance as needed)

Cover letter to parent contains:

- Purpose
- Itinerary
- Eating provisions
- Special clothes required

Consent form contains:

- Date of trip
- Departure time
- Return time
- Host information
- Cost
- Mode of travel
- Preferred physician
- Prescription drug information
- Other medical information
- Emergency telephone numbers
- Emergency medical aid release
- Space for signature and date

- Consent slips returned (all signed)
- Money collected
- Advance admissions and bus paid
- Supervisory helpers trained
- Provision made for nonparticipating pupils
- Cafeteria informed (fewer pupils eating)
- Other teachers informed (schedule changes)
- Class rosters prepared and distributed
- Principal clear on arrangements
- Bags for garbage and illness
- First aid kit
- Take trip and enjoy day
- Followup activities
- Evaluation completed

FIELD TRIP CONSENT FORM

(name of pupil) has my permission to participate in a field trip under the supervision and direction of *(name of teacher)* on the following date(s) *(fill in appropriately)*. The pupils will be leaving the school building at approximately *(time)* and will return at approximately *(time)*. The pupils will be traveling by *(mode)*. During this educational field trip the pupils will visit *(list all sites)*. The total cost of this field trip will be *(amount)* per pupil of which you are responsible for providing *(amount)*.

_____

Signature of parent or guardian   Date

SPECIAL INSTRUCTIONS

Preferred physician's name and telephone number:
_____

Prescription drugs: _____

Other medical information: _____

My home telephone number: _____

My business telephone number: _____
Name and telephone number of person to contact in the event I cannot be reached: _____

EMERGENCY TREATMENT RELEASE

As a parent or guardian, I authorize the treatment of the person named above by a qualified and licensed medical doctor in the event of a medical emergency. This authority is granted only after a reasonable effort has been made to reach me. I agree to assume responsibility for expenses incurred in the handling of this emergency

Signature _____ Date _____

REFERENCES

DuVall, Charles R. "Video Transcription and the Field Trip." *Social Education* 38:279–80; March 1974.

Knapp, Clifford E. "Conducting a Field Trip: Organizational Patterns for Instruction." *Science and Children* 8:26–28; September 1970.

Krepel, Wayne J. "Field Trips and the Secondary Student Teacher." *Teacher Educator* 8:27–30; Autumn 1972.

CHAPTER 3
IDEAS AND STRATEGIES

The idea of utilizing community resources for instructional purposes is not new. Long before society developed a system of formalized education, the community was the sole source of education, with each family responsible for rearing its children within the tribal pattern. Fathers taught their sons to hunt and fish and care for the family, while mothers taught their daughters to perform the many household tasks so essential for survival. Operating within this system the entire tribe or social unit also assumed some degree of responsibility for the training and rearing of the young. Thus the survival of the tribe depended upon the total use of community resources in the educational process. Even today, some primitive cultures follow these basic educational patterns.

With increasing social complexity and interdependence, much of the responsibility for educating or training the young has been delegated to institutional agencies. Today the school is the agency charged with the major responsibility for this task. Beginning in the home with preschool experiences, the educational process continues with kindergarten, elementary, junior high or middle school, senior high school, college, trade school, and various forms of adult education. These institutions are creations of the society they serve, designed to perpetuate the society.

USING COMMUNITY RESOURCES

Over the years, an artificial separation has grown up between the schools and the community (society). The expression, used by both teachers and parents, "Wait until you get out into the 'real world' and find out what it's really like" best illustrates this gap. Communication exists, but it needs reinforcement. The field trip is one method of strengthening the existing ties between the community and the school program.

Textbooks and other teaching materials often treat historical and social events and ideas in such a way that pupils cannot relate them to their own experiences. Students need examples from personal experiences to relate the issues and processes of the classroom instructional program to their day-to-lives as they are living them. They need concrete evidence that texts and materials are relevant and of value. They need to come to know that all persons are products of their past—of their traditions, customs, values, and social mores. They need to become aware of the influences of ancestors and of those who are presently shaping lifestyles. Thus the teacher's job becomes one of relating the community—local and world—to what is happening both inside and outside the classroom. The field trip offers a unique educational opportunity to demonstrate, in a concrete manner, the relationship between the school and the "outside world." It helps to make education a relevant process within the mainstream of the community and an integral part of the lives of all persons.

Locating Community Resources

In order to use community resources for field trips effectively and to have knowledgeable persons visit the classroom, the teacher must be able to locate these resources and match them to the needs of the instructional program. Several methods are possible. Individual teachers may compile their own resource lists. Schools or school districts may choose to maintain common lists. Teachers enrolled in certain workshops may develop area-wide lists as a cooperative venture within these programs.

We recommend that teachers within a school building or within an entire school district pool their efforts and create some type of common listing. One result of such planned cooperation is to present the educational program to the community as united rather than fragmented in efforts to use local resources. Another advantage was discovered by a school district that placed all the resources available to it on the computer. Revision of the list was much easier and changes were possible almost instantaneously (DuVall and Truex: 102–6).

SUBJECT-ORIENTED TRIPS

The following descriptions of teachers' ideas and examples of field trips have been drawn from the available literature. These suggestions are presented to share the ideas of others. The listing is merely illustrative; it is certainly not intended to be comprehensive. The only limitation on the number and variety of field trips is that imposed by the innovative practices of the classroom teacher.

As indicated earlier, field trips should bring about a renewed and continuing interest in moving the school and the community closer together in their shared goal of better education. These diverse activities should therefore result in more meaningful experiences for students enrolled in the educational program.

An organizational device to help pupils become acquainted with the route they will be traveling on a field trip is the trip board. This instrument can be tailored for any type of trip, from walking to long distance travel, and it can be adapted for almost any grade level or subject matter. Zeitz described it as a device that helps define the route and goals of the trip. It consists of one or more maps, pertinent questions concerning each site, space for illustrations (art), and extra space for doodling on the return trip. One map, usually adapted from a highway or city street map, gives the main route. Other maps may be of particular sites visited such as a factory or specific section(s) of a museum or an aquarium. Questions related to the site may be included on the same page with the map or listed on separate pages. All pages are then stapled to a piece of heavy cardboard to give the student a hard surface on which to write pertinent observations and answers to specific questions. Extra sheets should always be included for additional notes or doodling on the way home (Zeitz: 72, 74).

Art

Although crafts compete for considerable art time in the elementary classroom, painting and sketching can provide an exciting series of experiences that often result in an interesting product to take home, to show, and to explain. A good example is a field trip used as an introductory activity to the teaching of art. In this case a fourth grade teacher reported taking 90 students, accompanied by several other teachers, student teachers, and other supervisors, to a park on the outskirts of the city where the adults conducted some of the children on small group tours of a farmhouse, an adjacent summer kitchen, and a smokehouse. While the small groups were on their tours, other students sketched what they saw. The next day, after returning to school, the children were asked to sketch what they remembered and to enliven their drawings by adding dogs, cats, chickens, and cows to the scenes. In addition to working from memory, children referred to the sketches made on the field trip. The art work was extended further by introducing students to the use of tempera paint, applied with either brush or sponge (Lyon: 33).

Vukelich reported an innovative use of the field trip for young children. She took her group of preschoolers to a local ceramics laboratory where they made plaster of paris casts of their own hands. The most important feature of the visit was the children's use of several cameras to film the entire event. The children's pictures gave an added dimension to their experience, providing a different view of the trip and permitting many interesting followup activities, both from the perspective of clay modeling and plaster hand casts (Vukelich: 384–86).

Art teachers and science teachers should not overlook the advantages of cooperative planning to use art as a motivational tool in the study of astronomy and vice versa. Observation of the sky and stars is a natural way to teach children astronomy. Such observation may also be used as motivation for art activities. For many of today's pupils who live in urban areas where pollution hides all but the brightest stars, constellations remain much of a mystery. Writing of his concern for teachers unable to take students out of the city into the countryside to view the heavens and the "great masterpieces" of the constellations, Bondurant proposed a planetarium visit as an acceptable alternative. Such visits can inspire students to create artwork related to space. They can also help students relate one subject area to another and understand that many masters of painting and other forms of artistic expression found inspiration in the natural world around and over them (Bondurant: 32–34).

A group of secondary art students made a trip to sugar bush locations near Potsdam, New York. The students had planned the trip for some time, but because of the often-changing climatic conditions in the north country they were able to select a date only one day in advance. Since this was an art class, consisting of watercolorists and photographers, part of the preparations revolved around students' individual projects, including their observations and their ability to adapt their projects to the field trip site. During the trip some students were able to complete several paintings as well as thumbnail sketches, while others were not so productive. Thus individual differences in skill and motivation were most apparent as a result of this experience (Smith: 19).

Career Education

Immediately following the closing of school on Memorial Day, a group of agricultural students spent four days touring the state of Oklahoma visiting farms, plants, and companies. Since the main purpose was to familiarize participants with specific careers, students were able to talk with persons actually doing the jobs in which they had a particular interest. In addition to achieving its main objective, the trip had supplementary values. Among these, it created unity among the FFA (Future Farmers of America) chapter members, who engaged in cooperative planning, fundraising, and organizing (Applegate and Hampton: 278–79).

One of the most frequently leveled criticisms of career education is that it tends to be slanted toward the trades and the most popular professions giving little attention to the college work needed to prepare for some careers. Aumiller described an activity that helped children perceive time as it related to the distant future and their choice of careers. First of all, he wondered if children really understood college and what it can do for them, and questioned that they had any basis of comparison within their experiential background. Then, as a remedy for the problem, he proposed a field trip to a local college campus where pupils could participate in an average day on campus, with an opportunity to meet college students, tour the campus, and get a general feeling for the way in which higher education is conducted. Following such a campus visit, pupils realized that becoming a lawyer, an engineer, or a teacher requires a great deal of preparation and hard work that covers a span of at least four years. To be most beneficial to younger students, it is important to involve as many college students as possible in such an activity. Sites of particular interest might include a museum, an art gallery, a planetarium, or another "highlight" of the college visited. Similar experiences can be arranged through local trade union training programs, business colleges, and other institutions of postsecondary education (Aumiller: 69–70).

Handicapped

Bennion reported on two field trips—one in the fall and one in the winter—to help her class of deaf children develop their language skills. The fall trip, an overnight visit to a cabin in the hills, preceded by a short trip to a farm and a small town, was designed to build concepts of distance, seasonal change, and history. Since all the students were deaf and needed concrete experiences as well as instruction in self-expression, the objective was to develop their understanding and use of language. Before this first overnight trip, students marked the route, including all their rest and observation stops, on a state map to reinforce their map-reading skills. Immediately after returning from the trip, they began preparations for their winter excursion. In February the "snow trip" used the same cabin as in the fall, but for five days. Again, the preplanning paid off. No accidents occurred, few problems developed, and students had a valuable language learning experience. While Bennion's activity dealt with the handicapped, it certainly is applicable to all pupils, just as most of the field trips described in this publication are equally applicable to all special needs pupils (Bennion: 70–71).

Home Economics

For the home economics teacher a field trip to a museum can be a source of many creative experiences for a class. Museum displays can be used to help students integrate their studies as well as see the interrelatedness of classes and their everyday lives. For example, a display of peoples from other cultures gathering wild plants or hunting game can illustrate nutritional and dietary concepts, and the relationships between food and culture, family structure, value systems, and the level of technological development. For design students displayed objects can be a source of inspiration, providing ideas for innovative ways to apply line, form, texture, and color to textiles, clothing, interiors, and household objects. Using museum displays as models, students in clothing classes might create their own display, showing how various objects such as sad irons (solid flatirons), hemming birds (clamps for holding cloth), thimbles, and measuring equipment were used to produce and care for clothing in earlier times. Students of household equipment, historic and cross-cultural aspects of clothing and textiles, shelter and foods, can gain valuable knowledge by closely examining or, if possible, participating in museum cataloging work. Finally, students of home management might examine displays of household implements and materials, as well as household interiors, comparing them with their present-day counterparts. They might also compare past and present-day methods of food preparation, clothing care, and household cleaning (Schrank and Musa: 28–31).

The teacher interested in consumer education can find no more appropriate place to visit than the local supermarket. After studying such topics as unit pricing, nutrition labeling, merchandising displays, bulk packaging, and the psychology of impulse buying, the class can then apply them in the store. During the visit, the group can also discuss with the manager and other store personnel the consumer's responsibility in foodshopping as well as the cost of consumer carelessness and theft. If students obtain answers to the question "What can consumers do to ensure that they get the most for their money?" the field trip to the local supermarket has been a success (Consumer Affairs Editor: 11+).

Industrial Arts

As a method of observation, the field trip takes the teaching of concepts out of the theoretical classroom mode and brings it to the concrete level in the actual situation. The opportunity to make direct on-site observation is probably the most obvious advantage of the field trip over classroom experiences. This is especially true for the industrial arts. For such classes, the choice of site is, of course, determined by the type of class and site availability.

Teachers who wish to introduce and reinforce concepts of mass production, automation, assembly-line techniques, interchangeable parts, conveyor systems, quality control, and plant layout, and to observe workers performing tasks and machine tools in operation, should consider a trip to the appropriate site. Other possibilities to consider include visits to bridge construction sites, open pit mines (for removal of raw material), and new buildings under construction locally. Teachers of woodworking might find a furniture company, a toy company, or a packing company of interest. Drafting classes might consider visits to a blueprinting and enlarging operation, an architect's facility, a mapmaker, or the county surveyor's office (Muller: 27–29).

Language Arts/English

Combining the instructional areas of reading, language arts, and science into a field trip is an interdisciplinary approach that should be considered. Olson reported such an example, including the steps taken to involve students in planning and developing their own instructional program. In this case fifth graders made an all-day trip to the Indiana Dunes to observe evolution in action as exemplified at the lakeshore. It was the culmination of several shorter walking trips in which pupils developed their observational and note-taking skills. Preparations began in the fall with a reading exercise, a teacher-written story, "Nature's Time Machine," which explained the evolution of natural communities and described how northward movement of the lakeshore has left a sequence of examples of each stage in this process. As pupils used the story to plan an outline of what to look for on their trip, their reading skills developed. They also listened to weather forecasts and learned to evaluate what they heard, for if inclement weather appeared imminent, they must reschedule the trip. Before starting on any park trails, students had to identify their objective and their own position on their map. Therefore they developed mapreading skills as they learned to use the map as a guide in the park. When students have had the opportunity to work together, as in this experience, fatigue, attention span, and group behavior become less troublesome. Beginning with short trips, gradually increasing in length, the teacher can estimate the endurance level of the class. In addition, both teacher and students can develop many change-of-pace activities to help increase the endurance level (Olson: 26–28).

Scheduling field trips in the high school, where courses are departmentalized, can present many problems. One department solved this dilemma for the school by creating a course called "Field Trips" which was taught by members of the English faculty. Interdisciplinary in nature, the course required research on a variety of topics by each student. It stressed the interrelatedness of the school program and its many courses, and established and strengthened these relationships by the trips taken. Not only was the entire faculty aware of the trips and the days on which their schedules would be changed, but the students were also aware of their responsibility to "keep up" with their course work in classes missed while taking the trips (Workman: 283–85).

Mathematics

The final reminder from any teacher to students taking a field trip should be: "Take along your meters." In other words, each youngster should be equipped with a meter measuring strip. Ropa suggested that "the basic item is self-adhesive paper or vinyl which is quite inexpensive. . . . Most brands have a measurement grid on the backing paper to aid in cutting meter strips of equal width. Cut enough strips so each pupil has one. Do not remove the backing paper." (Or teachers might prefer to make measuring strips from heavy cord or clothesline.) As Ropa's trip progressed, students first estimated different objects—"shorter than a meter," "longer than a meter," or "exactly one meter." Then they confirmed these estimates by measuring. Ten volunteers, holding their meters end to end, became one dekameter. In the park the hectometer became a reality, followed by shouts of "Let's measure a kilometer!" And so the learning progressed, without using conversions, but actually experiencing the metric measuring system (Ropa: 78–79).

Music

Wessinger described a program she developed in Honolulu which involved working cooperatively with the high school band director. Her kindergarten pupils had been learning the rudiments of sound and through this developmental process had "discovered" the different sounds made by the various musical instruments. Beginning their study with noise and variations of audio-stimulation around the home (traffic noises, babies crying, doors slammming), they progressed to the concept that vibrations produce sound. Next they learned about vocal chords, both their own and others, and the way in which sound is produced. Then they created their own simple musical instruments (stringed boxes, primitive tom-toms, water-filled glasses, rubbed sticks), after which they formed their own band and realized that they needed a conductor to keep them together. This situation led to the field trip in which each child had the opportunity to lead the high school band in practice. First they lined the wall of the rehearsal room and heard the band in practice, "feeling" the vibration of the sounds created by talented older students. Then they had the opportunity to "lead" the band. Finally, they mingled with the players and handled the instruments. Through these activities the children developed a deeper sense of appreciation for music and for the talent and work necessary to make these specialized sounds (Wessinger: 31–32).

According to Finn, the integration of the community in the total school instructional program can be achieved by introducing local resource people to students. In the music program it can be accomplished by bringing in local musicians to play in the school orchestra as guest artists. Students can also be taken on field trips to hear local symphony orchestras or other musical performances. The strong association pattern of school-community involvement can be strengthened when students see their "guest artists" performing in the symphony or with other local groups. In addition, students can talk with persons engaged in music-related careers about the care and maintenance of their instruments. If there are musical instrument factories nearby, trips can be arranged to permit students to see the actual manufacturing process (Finn: 44).

Science

Thanks to the American Cetacean Society (ACS), Southern California pupils were provided a unique opportunity several years ago. During the months of December, January, and February, traveling very close to the continent, the gray whale, *Eschrichtius gibbosus*, migrates in small groups from the Bering Sea and Arctic Ocean to the warm southerly lagoons of Mexico, where the females give birth to single calves. Then, in March, April, and May, the herd begins its northward migration. An ACS-initiated program took pupils ranging from fourth grade through high school on half-day cruises to observe the whales. One of the program objectives was to develop a sense of conservation in students. We mention this venture as an example of the viability of using locally available resources to achieve educationally sound objectives. Each locality throughout the nation has its particular phenomena which can be used to the educational advantage of the instructional program. This example also illustrates how good community-school cooperation can provide a unique educational experience (Lande: 521).

Resourceful teachers will relate all facets of the field trip to the educational objectives, including making effective use of the time spent on the bus. Teacher- or student-devised bingo cards used for a science class, but adaptable to all subject areas, are an illustration. Developing such cards for class use can be a part of the planning phase. In addition to providing a valuable learning experience, the task is an activity in using research skills. For the science class the cells of each card contained pictures or words—cut from old texts, dictionaries, or free print materials—to encourage students to use several senses or only one sense. To provide variety to the game, the various cells should of course be changed around. Cards were laminated for reuse by subsequent classes and small adhesive labels were attached to the corner of each cell for marking during one use, to be removed or replaced before the next use. To play the game students marked their own cards as they discovered the individual items (Rathbone: 134).

Roberts described a 12-day trip taken by a group of 26 middle school students in Minneapolis to museums and fossil sites in six states. The students, who were enrolled in a paleontology class entitled "Can You Dig It?" returned from the trip with notebooks crammed with "exuberant journal notes" as well as many new and exciting discoveries. Anderson, the teacher, began preparations nearly a year beforehand. They included extra readings and classwork, local practice digs, making campsite reservations, filing permission slips, and obtaining the use of a school bus for the trip. En route to Mammoth Cave in Kentucky, their eventual destination, the students visited Chicago's Field Museum of Natural History. They also stopped at road cuts and designated fossil search sites, and limestone quarries in southern Indiana. Most of their discoveries were trilobites, the segmented, beetle-like marine animals which appeared on earth about 600 million years ago. The success of the trip encouraged the teacher to plan for a similar excursion in the future (Roberts: 80–82, 86).

When the annual May "vacation fever" struck one teacher's class, he capitalized on it to reinforce the teaching of physics by taking his students to an amusement park, where they related scientific physical principles to the park rides. First, the teacher developed a carefully defined set of educational objectives to accomplish this task. He spent two Sundays measuring and estimating distances, heights, and dimensions, and carefully timing rides, and a third afternoon acquiring the necessary electrical information with the help of park personnel. Then he prepared student booklets which included rules of conduct, a map of the amusement park, and information on the terminal goal—to conduct research on two rides and to complete the stated performance objectives of those rides. The booklets also contained a page of formulas and necessary conversion factors and a set of ten project sheets, each of which introduced one or two rides and listed specific performance objectives. Then, it was off to the amusement park for a full day of fun, measuring, and calculating. Followup sessions in class were a final aspect of the project (Kuczma: 20–21).

Baer, a Massachusetts teacher, described the use of national parks—in this instance Acadia National Park, Maine—as a field trip site. All members of his biology classes were permitted to apply for this fall trip. Because of vehicle and sponsor shortages, however, all students could not participate. Therefore, those believed most likely to profit from the experience were chosen. The selection process consisted of a written application with several questions specifically adapted to this particular experience. Students selected were responsible for obtaining assignments and keeping up with work they missed in other classes. On the trip they did population studies, made wildlife sketches, examined symmetries in organisms, and noted the impact of the many tourists who visited the park each year. In addition, each student was required to submit a miniproject which was used to illustrate the educational benefits of the field trip to parents, community members, and other interested individuals (Baer: 98–101).

A technique used for biology by a Kansas teacher can be adapted for a variety of field trip sites. In this case the teacher offered students the opportunity to concentrate their efforts on two topics of their choice (e.g., soils, reptiles, rodents, water, wildlife photography, and forestry). Six field trip sessions of approximately 90 minutes each were held concurrently by several instructors. Each group was limited to 20 students from a total enrollment of 75. Following the collection of samples and exhibits, the students ate sack lunches and then gathered to compare their data, take pictures of live specimens, discuss correct collecting techniques, and summarize their findings. These reports, shared throughout the semester, gave students background data and experience, and made the textbook topics come alive. Pictures, data, and slides made during the field trip augmented classroom instruction throughout the year (Highfill: 48–49).

Wiper used the museum as the site for a final examination for his human biology course, a practical course intended for noncollege-bound students. A school policy required a two-hour final examination. In order to comply with this requirement and to provide students an experience that would give them the maximum educational benefits, the teacher made arrangements for them to take the examination in the Museum of Science in Boston. Before the examination Wiper visited the museum and became thoroughly acquainted with the exhibits related to the course. Then he constructed the test questions based upon the course content and exhibits on human reproduction, nutrition, the respiratory and circulatory systems, medical history, a medical operation, and the "transparent" woman. On the day of the examination he gave each student a clipboard, several open-end questions, and a map of the museum identifying the exhibits. Earlier he had encouraged students to bring their class data books and offered them the option of working with a friend. During the examination, the instructor as well as museum aides were visible and available to help students if requested. As a result of his success with this process, the teacher had plans to repeat the trip and to expand the idea to other units of study (Wiper: 322).

Wurzelbacher reported a 28-day field trip to study the environment—camping for credit—covering 12 states and two Canadian provinces. The itinerary included such cities as Boston, Montreal, New York, Philadelphia, Quebec, and Washington, D.C.; Acadia and Fundy national parks; and places of special ecological significance. It also included an outstanding three-day canoe trip arranged by the Canadian Department of Youth and Tourism. On this tour students learned the value of teamwork and group responsibility through actual experiences. They also observed the relationship of people to their natural and created environment. Wurzelbacher's article contains an outline of the trip's budget (which would have to be drastically adjusted for inflation), lists of suggested personal and group camping equipment, and selected student observations of the experience. It also gives suggestions for a "shakedown" camping experience as a part of the preplanning and orientation sessions. This type of trip is an excellent idea for the adventurous teacher who wants to add excitement and imagination to the curriculum (Wurzelbacher: 341–43+).

Social Studies

Cemeteries, particularly those that have tombstones relating to the historic past, can be used to motivate children to study the history of their community. An Ohio teacher prepared herself for such a project by becoming familiar with the history of the local community and of the cemetery chosen for a field trip. As a part of the planning, the children established rules of conduct for visiting the cemetery. On the trip they developed their observational skills by noting dates of birth and death, family groupings, graves of war dead, and other aspects of life and death conveyed by the tombstones. In addition to developing learnings in history, they used mathematical skills to calculate lifespan. Learnings extended to the health curriculum with a study of epidemics, determined by noting that many deaths occurred during the same time period. Then, upon returning to school, the class visited the cafeteria to discuss food handling procedures with the personnel. As a result, students looked at the food handling permits and interpreted them as society's way of controlling the spread of diseases. Also, pupils were encouraged to talk at home with their parents about life and death so that parents would have the opportunity to share their thoughts on the matter. Thus, exploring the past, as detailed on tombstones, can add new dimension and meaning to the everyday lives of the children involved in the experience (Bassett: 94–96).

A teaching unit by O'Dowd focused upon the architecture of the many historic houses in the neighborhood of the school in which she taught on Staten Island. This is an excellent example of taking the common sights that children pass every day en route to school and making them a part of their learning experiences. Each morning, before the regular classes began, one teacher met with recent non-English-speaking arrivals from Santo Domingo, Colombia, Cuba, and India, as well as the other pupils in the class, to study the history and architecture of the homes. Some children were the sons and daughters of business and professional people, college professors, and civic leaders, while others were members of foster families. All the children shared the common experience of seeing and learning more about the cultural past of the community in which they lived. Resource persons visited the class. The children made special trips to a nearby vocational school where the teacher and his students gave an illustrated talk on construction. Finally, an architect accompanied the class on a combination walking-bus tour of the area. During this excursion, one homeowner welcomed the group with a personally conducted tour and an account of the house's long history. Classroom activities took the form of discussions and research, as well as making notebooks of pertinent material, illustrating architectural features of homes viewed on field trips, drawing pictures, taking photographs, preparing displays for bulletin boards, making Victorian mansion collages, and reliving the historic period of the homes through creative writing (O'Dowd: 137–39).

Walking trips offer opportunities early in the school curriculum to relate the school and community to the social studies program. In Waterbury, Connecticut, a walking trip at the beginning of the year acquainted the children of one school with the history of their community. It also helped them develop a spoken language facility since many students in the school had language and word development deficiencies. It served, too, as a means of teaching basic mapreading skills as the children explored the neighborhood. Teachers planned the project for a five-day (one school week) cycle, dividing the time as follows:

1st Day: Teacher planning—deciding area of concentration for the week

2d Day: Children's orientation—including a discussion of basic concepts, an exchange of information, a mapping activity, and the writing of key words and phrases in their journals

3d Day: Walking trip—making the trip with children following the route marked on the map

4th Day: Followup activities—displaying all samples, sharing experiences and observations

5th Day: "Pulling together"—repeating the walking tour, asking children to sketch their favorite site, and further sharing and recording the experience through a variety of expressions such as speaking, reading, writing, drawing, tape recording, labeling, and displaying (Vitone: 27).

Leeson described a different approach to eighth graders' study of Portland (Oregon), a requirement of that city's curriculum. The course emphasized three aspects of the city with social implications: how city people can expand friendships, features created by people that add or detract from a metropolitan environment, and suggested improvements for the future. Because third graders also studied Portland, they were involved in the eighth graders' project. Both student groups profited from the educational experience, learning with and from each other. Among the mutually beneficial activities—the older students prepared maps and projects which they presented to the younger children, and they acted as guides to the younger children on field trips. One third grader's comment probably best summed up the feelings of the entire group: "The reason I liked going this way is that it gives me someone to talk to and someone to ask questions of." (Leeson: 136).

A three-day trip that used two buses and four campers was an adventure in history shared by the eighth grade students taught by Bunselmeier and Galloway. The purpose of the trip was to study the history of the early gold-mining areas of California and Nevada. Before embarking on their adventure, the students planned the trip for an entire year—studying the history of the area and collecting facts. This account is but one example of using the history of the local area to motivate students, to make the subject live, and then of using the extended field trip as the culminating activity. One note of caution—when considering trips to abandoned mines, teachers should be sure to check safety factors of sites to be visited (Bunselmeier and Galloway: 52+).

The skill of letter writing can be combined with the study of history, as some Pennsylvania students discovered several years ago. Through corresponding with peers in Walpole, Massachusetts, students from Lancaster had the opportunity to learn firsthand about New England history. All year the students, carefully matched by their teachers, exchanged letters, relating to their eighth grade history course. The culmination of all of the letter writing was a visit by the Lancaster students to their Walpole pen pals for four full days. To finance this venture in cooperative learning, the Lancaster students and their parents spent many long hours raising the money required. The eighth graders' study of United States history was truly enriched by the correspondence and by the trip that closed the 400-mile gap and made history come alive (Blahusch: 39–41).

Multidisciplinary Trips

Glatthorn and Briskin reported on an alternative school program in Philadelphia in which the school first rented and later purchased a motor home. After the school established trip guidelines, interested groups applied for the use of the motor home. A committee set up for the purpose then screened the requests. The following are a few brief descriptions of some of the tours taken by different groups of students, parents, and interested staff members.

Art Tour. Students and a staff member toured New England museums, art schools, and art institutes. The group obtained information about schools, enjoyed many cultural experiences, and sketched and painted along the way both to and from New England.

Politics Tour. Visiting Washington, D.C., students and staff members met and talked with members of Congress and also did some lobbying.

Language Tour. During this trip the group stayed with French-Canadian families and tested their ability in conversational French in local restaurants.

Design Tour. Students and staff participated in the International Design Conference in Aspen, Colorado, visiting many sites of interest on the way west and on the return trip.

Among the points stressed on these trips were the necessity for good planning, early involvement of parents, establishment and enforcement of rules (all trips were coed), and preplanning for missed class work while on the road as well as planning for adequate study times. Needless to say, all trips had to have an educational focus—and the entire group had to keep this in mind at all times. One of the major benefits gained through the use of the motor home for educational travel was that it helped people learn how to get along with each other (Glatthorn and Briskin: 44–46).

Students can gain an understanding of the problems of the handicapped by visiting institutions where these persons are housed. Bernagozzi described the experiences of a third grade class that visited the elderly residents of a nursing home. The group prepared for its trip by discussing the problems of persons who can no longer take care of themselves, and by rehearsing a musical program. Because the home had no piano, the children took along a previously recorded piano accompaniment which they used for practice as well as for their performance of Christmas carols at the nursing home. When the children entered the room and saw the elderly on crutches, with canes, or in wheelchairs, their first reaction was one of total awe. The author felt that the pupils gained a great deal from this experience and that they provided the older people with a welcome relief from their daily routine. On the ride back to school, the children were quiet and contemplative. The understanding and compassion they exhibited for the problems of the elderly were different from the responses exhibited before the visit. Their experience reinforced the idea that there are many persons who are less fortunate than others. Discussions were therefore more meaningful following the experience of sharing their music with the residents of the nursing home (Bernagozzi: 29).

In the northern United States and Canada, winter is a reality, and any teacher contemplating the use of field trips as a part of the instructional program should be prepared to deal with this fact. Even so, winter can be an enjoyable and educationally rewarding time to plan and take a field trip. Serrin described one such excursion, an interdisciplinary activity for a group of fifth graders who spent all day outdoors in a park. Although its basic thrust was environmental education, the activity involved all areas of the curriculum. For example, it incorporated literature with reading and poems focused on the outdoors. Students learned to do research and to write reports on their observations as a part of the language program. Before the trip, the children received instruction in practical ways of coping with the winter environment, including building fires and keeping them going. They also received instruction in skiing. Food was limited to what each person could carry in a half-gallon milk container. Once in the park, students practiced such skills learned in class as finding an abandoned hermit's shack by using compass directions and starting a fire using a maximum of three matches. Not all the children experienced success and some occasionally needed help, but all learned from the outdoor activity. With appropriate planning and preparations, winter can become a special time to combine the classroom and the field trip to teach pupils needed skills and to make learning an enjoyable experience (Serrin: 102–4).

Visits to construction sites are another source of interest to students. These activities have implications for mathematics, career education, and other related classes. They must be modified to meet the availability of local construction, however; and they must be implemented when the teachable moment is at hand—that is, when the construction is under way. Usually it is necessary to obtain special permission to make an on-site visit, and this may sometimes be difficult because of insurance coverage and safety rules and regulations. Sites can be observed from public viewing places or from a distance, however. For instance, students can view a bridge under construction and make predictions about its height, length, and date of completion. Such predictions can be a useful way to teach estimation ratios and basic geometry. A later classroom visit from the construction supervisor or the design engineer can serve to establish the accuracy of student estimates (Zeitz: 76).

International Travel

Teachers contemplating travel with students to foreign countries must attend to special concerns not faced by those traveling within the continental United States. In addition to the usual arrangements involved in planning any field trip, there are matters of finances, transportation (both air and ground), selection of proper-type lodging accommodations, locally guided tours, baggage handling and weight limitations, passport and visa acquisition, health certificates and inoculations, and special clothing requirements to consider (Daniel). Therefore it is probably advisable to seek the counsel of a professionally trained travel agent who can work with the group from the trip's inception to its successful conclusion.

To make foreign travel as rewarding an educational experience as possible, the teacher should begin to work with the group well in advance of the trip. Preparations that help students develop an understanding of cultural differences and local customs of the nation(s) to be visited will not only make the trip more enjoyable for all involved—visitors and hosts alike—but they will also help avoid misunderstandings due to lack of awareness of different cultural values. To this end, discussions, guest speakers, the use of library facilities and other sources can be most helpful (Churchill).

The following brief descriptions of several international travel programs are examples of some of the tours that are available.

A fairly new program, designed around a "floating classroom," offers student leaders the opportunity to spend 20 days aboard a ship visiting many different ports. One hundred students can enjoy the experience of travel and association with their peers from all over the United States while visiting Mediterranean and Atlantic ports of call. They also attend classes in leadership skills and study cultural and historical perspectives of the area visited (National Association of Secondary School Principals: 19).

Friendship Ambassadors Foundation offers teachers in the performing arts the opportunity to sponsor international trips for their students. This organization has arranged many varied and interesting travel-performance itineraries for student groups over the past quarter of a century (Friendship Ambassadors Foundation).

A people-to-people travel program, stressing the role of people as goodwill ambassadors, is available for several areas of international study. Founded in 1956, the program is dedicated to world peace through international travel. It provides further evidence in support of the notion that teachers and organized student groups can profit educationally from trips to other countries. Bryant described a 1975 tour of music teachers during which doors to conservatories and academies that otherwise would never have been available to participants were opened. The tour covered Holland (Amsterdam), East Germany (Leipzig/Dresden), Austria (Vienna), the Soviet Union (Kiev), Hungary (Budapest), and Spain (Barcelona) (Bryant: 32–34).

SUMMARY

One purpose of this publication has been to stress the existence of a wide range of instructional resources available to teachers. From walking to flying, the local community and the world offer unlimited opportunities to teach by doing and observing firsthand. Because teachers are highly creative individuals, another purpose of this work has been to foster this creativity by suggesting ideas for broadening the scope of the educational program. The foregoing examples of field trip experiences represent only a diversity of suggestions.

A final suggestion is to view energy problems as a challenge for greater staff cooperation rather than as a deterrent to the use of the field trip. For example, while it may not be possible to engage a 60-passenger bus for one class, it may be possible for two classes to combine their efforts and double the effectiveness of the field trip. If school transportation is no longer readily available, the use of commercial sources should be considered. Furthermore, sites previously bypassed as groups went to more distant points may now warrant closer examination and use as possibilities for walking or bicycling excursions.

All forms of teaching and learning pose challenges to the teacher. With creative teaching, the field trip can be a valuable source to help students understand that they are a part of the local community as well as of the community of nations.

REFERENCES

Applegate, Leon, and Hampton, Gordon. "Summer Tour." *Agricultural Education Magazine* 49:278–79; June 1977.

Aumiller, Roy. "Kids on Campus." *Teacher* 96:69–70; April 1979.

Baer, Roy K. "Using a National Park for a Field Trip." *American Biology Teacher* 39:98–101; February 1977.

Bassett, Ruth. "Reading History from Tombstones." *Instructor* 80:94–96; April 1971.

Bennion, Leora. "The Whole Year Centered Around Our Trips." *Instructor* 83:70–71; October 1973.

Bernagozzi, Tom. "Spreading Christmas Cheer." *Early Years* 9:28–29; December 1978.

Blahusch, Charles. "Students Find On-Site History an Exciting Trip." *Momentum* 7:39–41; February 1976.

Bondurant, R. Lynn, Jr. "Planetarium Art: Using the Sky to Motivate Works of Art." *Arts and Activities* 74:32–34; September 1973.

Bryant, Celia M. "People-to-People: How Beautiful." *American Music Teacher* 25:32–34; September/October 1975.

Bunselmeier, Pat, and Galloway, Ray. "We Explored Early Mining Operations." *Instructor* 85:52+; October 1975.

Churchill, Jo Ann. "And You Shall Be an Honored Guest." Paper submitted to Institute of Certified Travel Agents (Wellesley, Mass.), 1979.

Consumer Affairs Editor. "How to Plan an Effective Field Trip." *Forecast for Home Economics* 24:11+; September 1978.

Daniel, Shirley. "Preparation for Travel: An Obligation of the Agent." Paper submitted to Institute of Certified Travel Agents (Wellesley, Mass.), 1974.

DuVall, Charles R., and Truex, Donald W. "Computerized Community Resources: A Data Bank for Planning Field Trips." *AEDS Journal* 7:102–6; Summer 1974.

Finn, Peter. "Making the Most of Community Resources." *Music Educators Journal* 63:44–47; March 1977.

Friendship Ambassadors Foundation (New York, N.Y.). Personal letter to authors from Administrative Director, dated January 14, 1980, with accompanying documentation.

Glatthorn, Allan A., and Briskin, Jon. "School on Wheels." *Today's Education* 62:44–46; May 1973.

Highfill, Kenneth. "Ideas for Student Self-Involvement in Environmental Field Studies." *American Biology Teacher* 39:48–49; January 1977.

Kuczma, Philip A. "Physics of an Amusement Park." *Science Teacher* 44:20–24; May 1977.

Lande, Rivian. "Whale Watching." *American Biology Teacher* 35:521–22+; December 1973.

Leeson, Jeanne Tellier. "Focusing on the Local Scene—Class Cooperation in Portland." *Instructor* 82:136–37; August 1972.

Lyon, J. "Painting: The Milieu." *Arts and Activities* 73:32–33; June 1973.

Muller, Warden B. "Make and Take, but Don't Forsake, the Field Trip." *Industrial Arts and Vocational Education* 58:27–29; September 1969.

National Association of Secondary School Principals. "International Student Leadership Program." *Student Advocate* 6:19; January 1979.

O'Dowd, Angela. "Focusing on the Local Scene—Exploring Staten Island Through Its Architecture." *Instructor* 82:137–39; August 1972.

Olson, Lynn. "Field Trips—Planning for Success." *Instructor* 81:26–28; June 1972.

Rathbone, Charlie. "Lookout Bingo." *Learning* 7:134; October 1978.

Roberts, Nancy. "Once upon a Trilobite . . . ." *Instructor* 88:80–82; March 1979.

Ropa, Adrienne. "Roll Out the Meters." *Instructor* 86:78–79; May 1977.

Schrank, Holly L., and Musa, Kathleen E. "The Museum as a Teaching Tool." *Journal of Home Economics* 70:28–31; March 1978.

Serrin, Barbara. "Why Not Winter." *Instructor* 87:102–4; January 1978.

Smith, Sherwood. "A Sugar Bush Trip." *School Arts* 75:18–19; December 1975.

Vitone, Sister Catherine. "Developing Language Through Field Experiences." *Momentum* 10:27; February 1979.

Vukelich, Carol. "A Trip to Take Cameras With." *Language Arts* 54:384–86; April 1977.

Wessinger, Barbara C. "Future Instrumentalists Visit a Band." *American Music Teacher* 23:31–32; January 1974.

Wiper, Harold. "A New Place for a Final Examination." *American Biology Teacher* 40:322; May 1978.

Workman, Brooke. "The Field Trip Course: Try It, You'll Like It." *Clearing House* 49:283–85; February 1976.

Wurzelbacher, Thelma. "Putting Environmental Education on the Road." *American Biology Teacher* 35:341–43+; September 1973.

Zeitz, Pearl. "Shaping Up the Class Trip." *Teacher* 96:72–77; March 1979.

Recommended Readings

Anagnosti, John. "Saturday Field Trips." *Instructor* 79:105; March 1970.

Britton, Robert A. "Fare Deals from Scheduled Airlines: A Primer for Migratory Geographers." *Journal of Geography* 77:136–40; April/May 1978.

Danilov, Victor J. "Museums as Educational Partners." *Childhood Education* 52:306–11; April/May 1976.

DeBlasi, Robert. "Cooperative Walk Through Time." *Science and Children* 16:8–9; April 1979.

Falk, John H. "Life in Early California: A New Approach to the Outdoor Field Trip." *Science and Children* 11:18–19; November 1973.

Gautier, Marjorie J.; Brown, Nancy; and Raisch, William A. "Gateway to Growth: St. Louis Adventure." *Educational Leadership* 35:384–89; February 1978.

Hoffman, Earl. "The Classroom Teacher and School Law." *Educational Horizons* 49:33–39; Winter 1970–71.

"Instructor Bicentennial Mini Grants." *Instructor* 2:50–64+; October 1975.

Jackson, Claudia, and Sepez, Lois-Ann. "Plan-Ahead Social Studies: Turn an Historic Walking Tour into a Working Tour." *Instructor* 88:60; August 1978.

Jurgs, Don W. "The Real World Is Out There." *Science and Children* 16:12; April 1979.

Kelsey, Kenneth W. "A Neighborhood Field Trip." *Science and Children* 16:14–15; April 1979.

Kidder, Cheryl. "Travel Abroad: Places to Go and People to See." *Journal of Learning Disabilities* 9:259–64; April 1976.

Kollauf, Paul D. "How to Set Up Field Trips and Get the Most from Them." *Industrial Education*, 38–39; September 1975.

Lee, David S. "Field Studies from a Rooftop: Monitoring Autumn Hawk Migration." *American Biology Teacher* 39:17–20; January 1977.

Lindemer, George C. "Historical Museums for Educational Enrichment." *Social Studies* 62:258–62; November 1971.

Mason, Jack L., and Troxel, Verne A. "University Students as Leaders for Field Trips." *Science and Children* 16:10–11; April 1979.

McGlathery, Glenn, and Hartmann, Martha N. "The Museum as a Teaching Resource: An Inquiry Approach." *Science and Children* 11:11–13; November 1973.

Mealy, Virginia T. "Invite-an-Expert Field Trips." *School and Community* 56:26–27; May 1979.

Midgett, Barry. "Tight Ship Trips." *Teacher* 97:90+; September 1979.

Orton, Peter, and Stevens, Joyce. "Survival in Boston." *Education Digest* 42:19–21; April 1977.

Pestrong, Raymond. "Geology in the Raw." *Journal of Geological Education* 27:155–56; September 1979.

Punke, Harold H. "Safety and Early Childhood Education." *Journal of School Health* 41:146–53; March 1971.

Rice, J. M. "Teaching by Travel: A School Excursion from Indiana to Virginia." *Forum* 18:20–30; 1894.

Stone, Adolf. "Field Trips, Catalysts for Senior Citizen Education." *Journal of Geography* 75:276–79; May 1976.

West, Robert Z. "Making a Bicentennial Visit to Philadelphia a Bell-Ringer." *Audiovisual Instruction* 21:6–8; April 1976.

Wood, David E., and Gillis, James C., Jr. *Adventure Education*. Washington, D.C.: National Education Association, 1979.

Wurzelbacher, Thelma M. "First Look at the Zoo." *Science and Children* 16:22–25; April 1979.

"5,000 Miles with a Special Education Class." *Ohio Schools* 53:20–23; November 14, 1975.